The Flourishing of Her Soul

A Journey Through Grief, Identity, and Divinity

Written by

Kymberley Clemons-Jones

The Flourishing of Her Soul: A Journey Through Grief, Identity, and Divinity

For quantity discounts contact the author at restorationlifecoach.com.

Published by Restored Life Publishing

Contact - kcjones@restorationlifecoach.com

ISBN-13: 978-0692725740

Cover Design by: DW Graphics LLC

Printed in the United States of America

CONTENTS

O Courage, My Soul

The Flourishing of Her Soul
A Journey Through Grief, Identity, and Divinity

"A life devoted to things is a dead life, a stump; a God-shaped life is a flourishing tree."
Proverbs 11:28, MSG

Introduction

Dear Friends, thank you for your interest in my work. I feel that poetry needs to get deep down into our souls to be of any value. It should have a pulse and a heartbeat, rhythm and timing. A great poem should be able to be read to music or better yet, create its own. I pray you are able to hear my heartbeat through the poetry in The Flourishing of Her Soul: A Journey through Grief, Identity, and Divinity. As you read, picture yourself journeying through these areas of your own life. Enjoy this journey from which none of us are exempt.

The Storm is Passing Over
(verse 1)

O courage, my soul, and let us journey on,
For tho' the night is dark, it won't be very long.
O thanks be to God, the morning light appears,
And the storm is passing over, Hallelujah!

Charles A. Tindley

GRIEF

Her heart sees dimly, and while trying to express all of its desires, chaos comes.

WIND-KISSED

The wind kissed my cheek this morning and
I asked what it wanted.

DANCING IN THE BLACK HOLE

There's a black hole in my heart
and dancing in the middle of it
is a whole lot of pain and agony.

My father and I are doing the tango.
Mama and me, we're doing the waltz.

Me and my big sister are doing the
electric slide through and
around our lives.

My brother, well, he crunks
chaotically in a battle for his life.

The men who touched me
show up doing some kind of satanic cult dance.

My slam-dancing boyfriend is there,
but he's found a new partner now.

Baby's daddy appears
flitting on- and offstage
like a ballerina confused by the next sequence of steps.

There's a black hole in my heart
humiliation and shame dancing together,
twirling up a storm.

TORTURE CHAMBERS

I dream of a torture chamber
where small shrinking passages
lead to overly spacious rooms
There is death
destruction
Devices that torture and kill
stretch and pierce
I am the unsuspecting
Sometimes with friends
other times alone
There is always danger
always fear
everywhere
a heart filled with dread
pumping
Someone's approaching
disguised in
a distorted mask
pulling me into the chamber

ANOTHER DAY

If I ran away today
Where would I go?
Everyone is here
All that I know.

If I ran away today
From the tragedies of life
Could I find a space
To flee from the strife?

If I ran away today
Would my heart feel relief?
Or would I be plagued
By my constant unbelief?

If I ran away today
Looking for that perfect place
Would I be missing
God's unbelievable grace?

If I stay where I am
Will God rescue me?
Help me to hold on
And help me to see?

If I stay where I am
I could hear God's booming voice
Or maybe a whisper
That would give me a choice.

I think I will stay here
If just for today.
The Lord will answer
This is what I pray.

BRIGHT ORANGE WITH WHITE POLKA DOTS

As I walk
with my umbrella hiding
my face
I am happy
for the rain.

I feel
sheltered from
the impinging world,
which ignores the
wisdom of pain
lining my face.

This umbrella
conceals
what I don't wish
to show
and what others would
dismiss anyway.

Downcast eyes,
fixed on my steps,
remain hidden by this
temporary sanctuary.

My daddy's worry lines are etched
in my forehead,
protected
from examination and analysis,
by this canopy
of bright orange with white polka dots.

The Flourishing of Her Soul

My mother's concern
that often shows
between my brows
has a chance to knit and
reveal
itself without fear of
contempt or scorn.

The life that has lived me
has a chance to
come out and
disclose
the pain and suffering
underneath the facade.

My destination comes upon me in
silence
while I
enjoy this solitude
and the
self-imposed separation
from those
who'd rather see my mask.

I arrive
crying on the inside.
My shield comes down
and the masquerade begins,
revealing itself
through smiles,
bright eyes, and
a forced vibrancy.

I hadn't even realized
that it had already
stopped raining.

IN THE GARDEN

I stand in the garden alone,
Recalling childhood friends who vowed to never leave my
side,
Who promised they'd always be an ever-present force in
my life.
These friends faded from my path long, long ago.
I remember them with great fondness.

I stand in the garden alone.
Images of loved ones surround me, grandmothers and
grandfathers long passed,
Memories of the good times and bad.
They never promised to stay,
But for some odd reason, I'd have bet my life they'd never
leave.

I stand in the garden alone,
Where the world is my enemy and
The terror never ceases.
The universe spins out of control and
I'm only a microcosm that no one sees.

I stand in the garden alone
because my family said, "I've got your back"
But it ended up being only
Sometimes or never.

Did Jesus feel like this when
He was in His garden?
He asked His friends to keep watch
While He had his nervous breakdown,

The Flourishing of Her Soul

But no one watched.

Sometimes I feel like Jesus, with sleeping frie
Who can't or
Don't
Understand,
Take vigil,
Pray, or keep watch.

Alone I stand in my garden.

The Storm is Passing Over
(verse 2)

O billows rolling high, and thunder shakes the ground,
The lightnings flash, and tempest all around,
But Jesus walks the sea and calms the angry waves,
And the storm is passing over, Hallelujah!

Charles A. Tindley

IDENTITY

Her mind is always racing, trying to rationalize the
emoting of her heart.

BODYFREE

My body's craving to be free
free from sickness
and free from pain,
free from guilt
and free from shame,
free from anger
and free from fear,
free from blame
and free from tears
Free to feel as I want
and love as I must,
free to give without strings,
to connect on a higher plane,
free to see what the rightcous see
and to use all of me
free to lose control
free to dance
free to sing
free to shout
free to Praise . . .
Yeah . . . free to Praise!
My body's craving to be free
Feeling trapped inside a corpse,
Limited by my flesh.
The Light is
restricted by the darkness
So I stop for a Word,
pause for an anointing,
wait for deliverance!

FROM DAUGHTER TO MOTHER

I remember when you showed me baby pictures
and told me I almost died at birth.
You told me I was "extra" special.
You poured out love from deep within your heart.

I remember when you parted my hair
and strategically placed Dixie Peach
in each designated spot before you would braid it.
You poured out love from deep within your heart.

I remember when I dressed up in your pearls and heels
and you just smiled and laughed.
You were probably thinking about your days past.
You poured out love from deep within your heart.

I remember when you would tell me to
sit up straight, hold in my stomach, smile
and how to stand so my one bowleg wouldn't show.
You poured out love from deep within your heart.

I remember when you picked me up early from school.
Granddaddy had passed and we were leaving for down
south.
You were so strong for me.
You poured out love from deep within your heart.

I remember when I walked home in a blizzard.
You scolded, "You should have stayed on that broken-
down bus."
Then you sat me down by the heated oven and massaged
the cold away.
You poured out love from deep within your heart.

The Flourishing of Her Soul

I remember when my legs would swell before our eyes.
The doctor said, "Growing pains."
You used that green alcohol mixed with aspirin and
rubbed away for two years straight.
You poured out love from deep within your heart.

I remember when I was at the altar, crying in pain,
and God gave you healing power.
The racking ache in my back has never returned.
You poured out love from deep within your heart.

I remember when you came to help me with your first
grandson.
You were supportive, never overbearing.
You allowed me to be a mother, all by myself.
You poured out love from deep within your heart.

I remember when we would discuss the love of God,
healing,
and the miracles of life.
You helped mold me into the woman I am today.
You poured out love from deep within your heart.

You've given me the gift of love,
the gift to love and to be loved
and to glorify God through my love.
And now, Mom, I pour out love to you from deep within
my heart.

ENCOUNTERING MYSELF

Sometimes I have visions of myself in a parallel universe.
I see Her walking down a street almost identical to mine.
As I walk, She walks, but there's something different
about Her.
She has light steps
but my steps are heavy with fatigue.
She smiles at all who pass Her way
but my eyes are cast low, seeing nothing but the concrete
before me.
She notices the gardenias in the neighbor's front yard
while their hue is lost on me.

Sometimes I have visions of myself in a parallel universe.
I see Her walking down a street almost identical to mine.
As I walk, She walks, but there's something different
about Her.
She sees the bluebird fly to the tree, singing songs of Zion
while
I'm silently enraged at the beauty of its song.
She can't wait to reach Her destination because there
she'll find joy, peace, tranquility, and abounding grace.
I slow my pace, wanting to savor what piece of sanity I
have left before I get - there.
She finds love and love finds Her at every bend, and I just
wonder where all the love has gone.

Sometimes I have visions of myself in a parallel universe.
I see Her walking down a street almost identical to mine.
As I walk, She walks, but there's something different
about Her.
I wonder if we'll ever meet, me and She.

I wonder . . .

The Flourishing of Her Soul

Meanwhile, I try to be more like Her because I like how
She walks.
I begin to walk to the rhythm of my new beat, or is it Her
beat?
I smell the tulips as they wave at me when I stroll by
and I even wink at cuties when our eyes briefly meet.

I had light in my heart when we collided, me and She.
You see, I was looking at a bluebird, high in the sky,
flying effortlessly across the setting sun when it suddenly
happened.
We both giggled like two schoolgirls, gave each other a
knowing look, and kept walking.

No longer in a parallel universe
She is now safely, securely, and joyously in Me.

INSPIRATION

Truly inspiring speech flowed through
The mouths of these beautiful women,
Stimulating the minds of those who bothered
To listen and take their noses
Out of their drinks.

The enlightened heard and understood
The beauty they bestowed,
The havoc they wreaked,
The wrath they imparted.

Light permeated the room,
Truth hanging in the air like smoke
Without the stench.

Picturing myself in the midst of it all
Inspired me,
Enlivened me,
Stirred me,
Drove me to mad dreams,
All of them a poem in the making,
Prompting me to write in my sleep as I always do.

Words slipping and sliding
Through my brain like those
Cartoon characters who run into oil
And can't regain control.
Legs flying,
Arms soaring,
They hold their breath,
Afraid to breathe
'Cause if they breathe, they will surely fall.

The Flourishing of Her Soul

Phrases and words leaving imprints on my mind,
On my heart,
On my soul,
Like the hieroglyphics of my people recording history
For all who dare to seek clarification,
Illumination and explanation.

The lexis of my ancestors imparts
Wisdom to my mind,
Flowing like the great Niger River over the cracks
And crevices embedded in my foundation.

Poetry was in motion in my dreams,
Leading me further into my destiny,
Further into myself.

Life is.
Let it be.

YOUR'E ALL THE ME I NEED

Lord, it's true
I really do think about myself entirely too much
The world revolves around ME
I spend so much time thinking about
What I'll eat
What I'll wear and
What I'll do
Tomorrow
Worrying about my schedule
My lack of time
Worrying about work
And getting promoted
Worrying about my relationships
And who will love me
Worrying whether I'll be able to write
That next line
Lord, it's true
I'm a bit self-centered
Okay, maybe more than a little bit
Everything's centered around what
Makes me happy
What makes me sad
What makes me angry
What makes me sane
What motivates me
It's all about me
Isn't it?
How do I have time to do anything
With my mind always worrying
And wondering about the next thing
I'm going to do
Or the next thing I'm going to say
The next thing I'm going to strive for

The Flourishing of Her Soul

The next thing I swear I'll die for
My Lord, it's true!
The world does revolve around me
How egotistical of me
How trite
How shallow of me
Here we go again
Me, me, me
Lord, it's time to focus on You
And stop thinking about me
After all, you've got it going on!
Why worry when you take care
Of all my needs and
My desires
Thank you God for the turnaround
I know, now, Lord
You're all the me that I need.

The Storm is Passing Over
(Verse 3)

The stars have disappeared, and distant lights are dim,
My soul is filled with fears, the seas are breaking in.
I hear the Master cry, "Be not afraid, 'tis I,"
And the storm is passing over, Hallelujah!

Charles A. Tindley

DIVINITY

God's calling. Are you listening?

PEACE, BE STILL

When life is cruel and damaging and you don't know what
to do
Peace, Be Still
God will come through

When you're broken, beat up, torn and the answers are
nowhere to be seen
Peace, Be Still
On God you can lean

When the bright skies grow dark and your pain doesn't
seem to end
Peace, Be Still
God's mercy is great and your heart God will mend

When your smiles have faded and your face shows more
than your years
Peace, Be Still
The Lord will dry your tears

When love seems to elude you and laughter ceases to exist
Peace, Be Still
Pray to God Almighty and God will assist

When you feel you are all alone and that no one really
cares
Peace, Be Still
God's answer will come quickly and your thoughts God
will repair

Whatever your circumstances and whatever your plight
Peace, Be Still
And don't lose sight

God is your comfort, your companion, your friend
Peace, Be Still
On God you MUST depend

JUST SAY I LOVE YOU

The passion burns within me every day
The longing to break free and love the world as it is
Just wanting to love everybody for who they are
For their contributions—large and small
Just wanting to say "I love you"
Not only to the ones who I hold close
But to the sister walking the streets, trading a connect for
a dollar
Or the brother pushing the corner's crack
Just saying "I love you" might make a difference
If not to them, then maybe to me
Love's eternal
Even after the words are gone
Faded into the air and a part of the past
Its mystery lives on forever
Penetrating through hard hearts and seeping
Into the dark places where light may have never existed
Love is God
Resonating at the same frequency
Saying "I love you" is saying God loves you
I love you, I love you, I love you
Shout it from the hills on high
Sing it from the valleys below
Feel it from the depths of your soul
Let it penetrate through your veins
And let it give birth to a life of light,
Of joy, of passion, and of peace
Just say "God loves you"
Just say "Peace"
Just say "Light"
Just say "Love"
Just to say "I Love You"

I LOVE YOU, MY NUBIAN PRINCE

My heart is full of joy
and full of love, my
Nubian Prince.

When you trod upon the brown
earth with shoeless feet,
I loved you.

While you hunted for food
with the strength of the gods,
I thought about you and your return.

During our tribal dance . . .
oh, how I loved to see you
in your beautiful colors and
see you dance with rhythmic grace.

And Now . . .

My heart is full of joy
and full of love, my
Nubian Prince.

When you stand with soled feet upon
the hardened ground,
I love you.

While you work the endless day
with boundless determination,
I anxiously await our reunion.

Our slow dance . . .
oh, how I love to feel your body

The Flourishing of Her Soul

simply and affectionately saying
you're mine.

You are my Nubian Prince.
Forever shall you reign and
be filled with the blood of your
noble ancestry and of God.

RAIN FALLING ON FLOWERS

Rain falling on flowers
Pit, pat, pit, pat, pit, pat
Like holding hands on a spring day
Like earth after a fresh rain
A brief shower in the dead of summer heat

Rain falling on flowers
Pit, pat, pit, pat, pit, pat
Like the melodic rapture of an ocean wave
Like freshly cut grass in the fall
A gentle caress down my back

Rain falling on flowers
Pit, pat, pit, pat, pit, pat
Like leaves cascading down in the autumn air
Like a warm, steamy bath with lavender bubbles
A warm breeze blowing gently over the windowsill

GOD, USE MY HANDS

God, use my hands
To write your words
so that others may be blessed
To transcribe your love
for all generations to see
To deliver your message
for all to hear

God, use my hands
To do good deeds
for those in need
To proclaim your mercy
to all that grieve
To convey your grace
to all who believe

God, use my hands
To testify
and bring others to you
To bless your name,
the name that is first among all others
To share your peace
to those who need it most

God, use my hands
To wipe away the tears
of a weeping child
To hold the hand
of a lonely man
To caress the face
of a grieving widow

The Flourishing of Her Soul

God, use my hands
To hug the girl
stricken with cancer
To care for the boy
who's been beaten
To heal the woman
who has been scarred for life

God, use my hands
To be your servant
To perform your miracles
To do your will

BLESSINGS FLOW FREELY

Blessings flow freely
All around us is God
On High Ridge Road
Where trees line the streets
Saluting all who enter
Some arching over the road
Protecting it from all
Ugliness
Serenity is here
Peace lives here
The sun shines brightly
Casting shadows of life on the
Other side
Cotton clouds invite you
To rest your head and hearts
New Canaan
Holy Land
Lawns are littered with colorful petals
The nectar so sweet
Red and brown leaves fall to the grass
Sheltering God's smallest creatures
Pussy willows stand at attention
Waving to those who pass
There's peace all around us
Beauty in the red clay crevices of rock
That line the landscape
Blessings flow freely
All around us is God

PRAISE

As I bow my head and knees
I free my palms,
Letting the wells of praise
Extend up to You.

I free my heart from
This web of flesh
Exposing myself to
Your glory and compassion.

Droplets of white and yellow energy
Dance in place in my hands
Spiraling, circling, waiting for direction,
Waiting for You to direct the rays of light.

The Storm is Passing Over
(Verse 4)

Now soon we shall reach the distant shining shore,
Then free from all the storms, we'll rest forevermore.
And safe within the veil, we'll furl the riven sail,
And the storm will all be over, Hallelujah!
Hallelujah! Hallelujah!
The storm is passing over,
Hallelujah!

Charles A. Tindley

Works Cited

The Message Bible: The Bible in Contemporary Language,
Eugene H. Peterson. NavPress, 2002. *BibleGateway.com,*
https://www.biblegateway.com/versions/Message-MSG-
Bible/

Tindley, Charles A. (1905). *Charles Tindley's Soul Echoes:
A Collection of Songs for Religious Meetings, No. 2 #4.*
Public Domain.

www.ingramcontent.com/pod-product-compliance
Lightning Source LLC
Chambersburg PA
CBHW021945040426
42448CB00008B/1247